Life with Hope
12 Step Workbook

Life with Hope

A Return to Living Through
the 12 Steps and the 12 Traditions of
Marijuana Anonymous

12 Step Workbook

Marijuana Anonymous World Services
5551 Hollywood Blvd #1043
Hollywood, CA 90028-6814
United States
+1.800.766.6779
www.marijuana-anonymous.org
Published by A New Leaf Publications, Walnut, CA 91789
www.anewleafpublications.org

ISBN: 978-0-97657-791-1

∞ This paper meets the requirements of ANSI/NISO Z39.48-1992 (Permanence of Paper).

This publication is not intended as a substitute for the advice of health care professionals.

In the process of being reissued in 2020, *Life with Hope 12 Step Workbook* has undergone minor editing updates and been retypeset.

The Twelve Steps and Twelve Traditions of Alcoholics Anonymous have been reprinted and adapted with the permission of Alcoholics Anonymous World Services, Inc. ("A.A.W.S."). Permission to reprint and adapt the Twelve Steps and Twelve Traditions does not mean that Alcoholics Anonymous is affiliated with this program. A.A. is a program of recovery from alcoholism *only*—use of A.A.'s Steps and Traditions or an adapted version in connection with programs and activities which are patterned after A.A., but which address other problems, or use in any other non-A.A. context, does not imply otherwise.

28 27 26 25 24   15 16 17 18 19

Printed in the United States of America
Hazelden Publishing
Center City, Minnesota 55012
hazelden.org/bookstore

Contents

Preface.. vii

How It Works.. ix

Step One... 1

Step Two... 6

Step Three... 9

Step Four.. 13

Step Five... 28

Step Six.. 31

Step Seven... 38

Step Eight.. 42

Step Nine... 46

Step Ten.. 48

Step Eleven... 51

Step Twelve... 55

Preface

This Step Workbook is the result of a cumulative effort by the worldwide fellowship of Marijuana Anonymous (MA). For years, sponsors adapted the worksheets from other Twelve Step groups, substituting language and ideology. Beginning in 2002, MA members began discussing the need to create our own companion to *Life with Hope*, MA's basic text, to help us navigate our way through the Steps.

At the Marijuana Anonymous World Service Conference in Orange County, California, USA, in May 2004, a motion was passed to begin this important work. It was agreed that each MA district (at the time there were twelve, how fortuitous) would focus on one Step and the Literature Committee would ultimately edit and assemble the worksheets into a cohesive workbook. This Step Workbook is the result of those efforts. It took four years and countless marijuana addicts to accomplish this task.

You can write directly in this book, couple it with a notepad, or use a computer. We have but one request before you begin: Please do this work with the guidance of a sponsor or spiritual advisor. As with recovery, this work is not intended to be done alone. Success depends on us sharing the process with others.

You are about to embark on a life-changing journey with the support of the fellowship of Marijuana Anonymous, your sponsor, and your Higher Power. Behold the miracles.

Thank you for allowing us to be of service.

Marijuana Anonymous World Services
Literature Committee

How It Works

The practice of rigorous honesty, of opening our hearts and minds, and the willingness to go to any lengths to have a spiritual awakening are essential to our recovery.

Our old ideas and ways of life no longer work for us. Our suffering shows us that we need to let go absolutely. We surrender ourselves to a Power greater than ourselves.

Here are the Steps we take which are suggested for recovery:

1. We admitted we were powerless over marijuana, that our lives had become unmanageable.
2. Came to believe that a Power greater than ourselves could restore us to sanity.
3. Made a decision to turn our will and our lives over to the care of God, *as we understood God.*
4. Made a searching and fearless moral inventory of ourselves.
5. Admitted to God, to ourselves, and to another human being the exact nature of our wrongs.
6. Were entirely ready to have God remove all these defects of character.
7. Humbly asked God to remove our shortcomings.
8. Made a list of all persons we had harmed, and became willing to make amends to them all.
9. Made direct amends to such people wherever possible, except when to do so would injure them or others.
10. Continued to take personal inventory and when we were wrong, promptly admitted it.
11. Sought through prayer and meditation to improve our conscious contact with God, *as we understood God*, praying only for knowledge of God's will for us and the power to carry that out.
12. Having had a spiritual awakening as the result of these steps, we tried to carry this message to marijuana addicts and to practice these principles in all our affairs.

Do not be discouraged; none of us are saints. Our program is not easy, but it is simple. We strive for progress, not perfection. Our experiences, before and after we entered recovery, teach us three important ideas:

- that we are marijuana addicts and cannot manage our own lives;
- that probably no human power can relieve our addiction; and
- that our Higher Power can and will, if sought.

Step One

We admitted we were powerless over marijuana,
that our lives had become unmanageable.

With the First Step we begin the recovery process. Working this Step enables us to move forward through the Twelve Steps of Marijuana Anonymous (MA). We may now find it useful to carefully examine some of our old beliefs, ideas, thoughts, and behaviors.

Step One is about honesty, our most helpful ally to a successful Step One. With the practice of this principle, we can face the reality of our addiction.

Step One is about admitting that we are powerless over marijuana, that our lives have become unmanageable. We suggest exploring the following activities and questions, and writing out your answers, allowing for reflection, discovery, and discussion with your sponsor.

Getting Started

- Begin reading *Life with Hope* through Step One. Note passages that are meaningful to you and statements or words that you don't understand.
- Look up dictionary definitions of the words you didn't understand.
- Look up the words *powerless* and *unmanageable* in the dictionary; write out the definition(s) that you find significant, and write what each word means to you in the space below.

Powerless

Unmanageable

- Review Step One in *Life with Hope* with your sponsor or a trusted fellow MA member.

Write a History of Your Marijuana Use

Write a detailed history of your marijuana use. Use extra page(s) as necessary. While writing, include answers to the following questions:

- What early life experiences led me to using?
- How did I feel the first time I used?
- What were my feelings over time as I continued to use?
- Did marijuana turn on me and, if so, when?
- What was my life like during my last sixty days of using?
- What brought me to Marijuana Anonymous?

Recall Experiences in Which You Were Powerless over Your Marijuana Use

1) How did I try to control my using?

2) How did my marijuana use keep me from realizing my potential?

3) How did my marijuana use keep me from doing what I wanted to do with my life? Do I think I can control other people, places, and things? Explain:

4) Where in my life am I powerless?

5) Where in my life do I have power?

Explain How Your Life Is Unmanageable

6) Did I make deals with myself that I was unable to keep? If so, explain:

7) What are some triggers that cause me to crave marijuana?

8) Have I ever experienced confusion, paranoia, and fear associated with my using? If yes, explain:

9) Was I withdrawn and isolated? If yes, explain:

10) Was I brought to the depths of despair and hopelessness? If yes, explain:

11) How was my life unmanageable when I was using? How is it unmanageable today?

Denial, Surrender, Honesty, and Acceptance

12) How have I been living "the fantasy of functionality"?

13) Am I done with the idea of being able to use again? If no, explain:

14) Do I blame the world or others for my problems? If yes, explain:

15) What does *surrender* mean to me?

16) Has my way of life been working for me? Explain:

17) Am I still looking for a way to control my using? If yes, explain:

18) Am I ready to admit that I am powerless over marijuana and that my life has become unmanageable? Explain:

Discuss your First Step work with your sponsor or a trusted fellow MA member.

Some say that Step One is the only Step we are asked to work "perfectly." Others say we need only work the *first half* of the Step "perfectly." We do that when we admit, accept, and surrender to the fact that we are powerless over marijuana.

When we can do that, and accept that our lives have become unmanageable, we are ready for **Step Two**.

Step Two

*Came to believe that a Power greater than
ourselves could restore us to sanity.*

Step Two is about open-mindedness, change, and hope. We consider trusting a Power greater than ourselves (and greater than our obsession with marijuana) that can help us deal with everyday life. We define *insanity* as repeating the same behaviors over and over again while expecting different results.

It is not necessary to acquire a major God Consciousness to be able to cease using. All we need is to maintain an open mind and a hopeful heart. *Higher Power* means different things to different people. There is room in Marijuana Anonymous (MA) for all beliefs, or none. Each of us finds a Power that works for us. Some of us draw strength and support from the fellowship. We begin to see that a Power greater than ourselves could do for us what we could never do alone.

Getting Started

- Read Step Two in *Life with Hope*. Note passages that are meaningful to you and statements or words that you don't understand.
- Look up dictionary definitions of the words you didn't understand.
- Look up the words *believe*, *restore*, and *sanity* in the dictionary; write out the definition(s) that you find significant, and write what each word means to you in the space below.

Believe

Restore

Sanity

- Review Step Two in *Life with Hope* with your sponsor or a trusted fellow MA member.

Recall Experiences of Insanity

1) What are some examples from my life of repeating the same behaviors over and over again and expecting different results?

2) Do I have thoughts of using again someday, even though I need or wish to stop using? Explain:

Examine Beliefs of a Power Greater Than Ourselves

3) What is my concept of a Power greater than myself?

4) Can I become open-minded to a new concept of a Power that works for me? Explain:

5) How can I focus on using a Higher Power to benefit my recovery?

Becoming Open-Minded

6) Has a lack of open-mindedness contributed to my reaching a bottom? Explain:

7) Am I ready to accept and/or choose a Power greater than myself that is positive, powerful, and with which I am comfortable? Explain:

8) Do I believe a Higher Power can do for me what I could not do alone? Explain:

Discuss your Second Step work with your sponsor or a trusted fellow MA member.

Welcome to **Step Three**.

Step Three

Made a decision to turn our will and our lives
over to the care of God, **as we understood God.**

In Step Two, we examined our concept of a Higher Power. The program of recovery can work for anyone who can accept a Power greater than him- or herself.

Step Three doesn't say, "We turned our will and our lives over." Rather, it suggests that we "made a decision" to do so. The idea of turning our will and our lives over to the care of a Higher Power can seem impossible to some of us. However, it can be done gradually, over time. This is possible when we become willing and have faith. What is important is that we start the process.

By staying in the present, we release the past and let go of the future. Doing so helps us relinquish our self-will. Many of us found that simply making this decision opened us up to a spiritual connection. This decision was an act of faith in and of itself.

For some of us, our faith started to grow as a direct result of our abstinence from marijuana. Others of us had to "act as if." We find that praying for willingness often helps.

Even if we do not understand or feel connected to a Higher Power, it is possible to work Step Three. To release our self-will, we make a decision to turn our will and our lives over to the *care* of a Higher Power. We let go and let God, *as we understand* (or don't understand) *God.*

Getting Started

- Read Step Three in *Life with Hope.* Note passages that are meaningful to you and statements or words that you don't understand.
- Look up dictionary definitions of the words you didn't understand.
- Look up the words *decision, will, acceptance,* and *faith* in the dictionary; write out the definition(s) that you find significant, and write what each word means to you in the space below.

Decision

Will

Acceptance

Faith

- Review Step Three in *Life with Hope* with your sponsor or a trusted fellow MA member.

Review the Third Step Prayer in *Life with Hope*

1) What, if anything, about this prayer works for me?

2) What, if anything, about this prayer do I resist?

3) Write your own version of this prayer, using as little or as much of the original as you choose.

Willingness versus Willfulness

4) What does *willingness* mean to me?

5) How does self-will affect my life?

6) Am I willing to be open to the idea of surrendering my will to the care of a Higher Power? Explain:

7) What stands in the way of my willingness, if anything?

8) Do I try to control people, places, and things? Explain:

9) Do I blame myself when I am not successful at doing so? Explain:

10) Have I tried to stop using marijuana through self-will? Explain:

11) Was I successful? Explain:

12) If not, why do I think that is?

Understanding the Care of a Higher Power

13) Do I have faith that my Higher Power can relieve my obsession with marijuana? Explain:

14) If not, do I have the willingness to "act as if" a Higher Power could do so? Explain:

15) Where in my life do I believe my Higher Power can take care of me?

16) Where, if anywhere, do I feel my Higher Power cannot take care of me?

17) Where in my life right now do I feel my Higher Power is taking care of me?

18) What does turning my will and my life over to the care of a Higher Power mean to me?

19) What fears do I have about turning my will and life over to the care of my Higher Power?

Discuss your Third Step work with your sponsor or a trusted fellow MA member.

Welcome to **Step Four**.

Step Four

Made a searching and fearless moral inventory of ourselves.

Now that we've been honest enough to take Step One, open-minded enough to take Step Two, and willing enough to take Step Three, we are ready for Step Four. Before we start this Step, it is important to ask what it is that we want from recovery.

Step Four does take courage. It begins the process of learning who we are. Many of us feared beginning this Step, but once we did the work, we found it was less difficult than we had imagined. The inventory is a detailed description of our character challenges, or defects of character, removed of judgment. Remember, it is an inventory; no action other than writing is required.

While we look at our character challenges and wrongs in Step Four, many of us found it helpful to examine our character assets as well. We encourage you to look at and list all aspects of your character in this Step. As you work through this process, you will likely gain a greater understanding and acceptance of the person you have been, and see the potential of the person you are becoming.

Taking this inventory is not a thinking exercise; it's a writing exercise. As you work on your inventory, try not to leave anything out because of shame, fear, or embarrassment. What you record is between you, your Higher Power, and your sponsor or other trusted person with whom you share this Step. We find that the more thorough and honest we are, the better results we get from this Step. Remember, we are only as sick as our secrets. Ask your Higher Power for help every time you sit down to write. There is no rush. We have found the rewards to be substantial.

Getting Started

- Read Step Four in *Life with Hope*. Note passages that are meaningful to you and statements or words that you don't understand.
- Look up dictionary definitions of the words you didn't understand.

The inventory suggested in *Life with Hope* (and this workbook) is really five separate inventories: Resentment, Fear, Sex, Secrets and Other Issues, and Assets. Each inventory is unique, and it is suggested that you do them one at a time, in the order set out in the pages that follow. Included are templates that might be helpful when doing this Step; we suggest that you make several copies of each before beginning, if you choose to use them.

These inventories may be handwritten or done on a computer. If writing by hand, have plenty of paper, or a notebook, and a quiet place to work. For many of us, writing by hand is more intuitive and less from reasoned thinking, which is best avoided here. Some find it helpful to use a computer when doing this work. Whatever our preference, the reward is release from the past and freedom from the pain that has enslaved us.

Before beginning this inventory, we recommend an exercise to facilitate openness and willingness. For many of us, this means a prayer to a Higher Power. Here's an example:

> *Higher Power, please bring to mind all of my resentments (fears, memories of sexual misconduct, etc.) that I need to look at in this inventory.*

The exact words we choose aren't as important as saying the words with a spirit of openness. Many of us have found that saying the prayer out loud is helpful. If we just relax and ask for help, it's amazing how freely the information we need to look at will flow onto the paper.

Three things to remember: (1) Stay focused. (2) Pray. (3) Keep writing!

- Review Step Four in *Life with Hope* with your sponsor or a trusted fellow MA member.

We are ready to begin.

Resentment Inventory

We usually begin with the Resentment Inventory, which is generally divided into four columns. It is strongly suggested that we complete one column at a time, from top to bottom (going onto several sheets if necessary), before beginning the next column. In other words, we list all the people, institutions, and principles that we resent in **COLUMN 1** before looking at anything in **COLUMN 2** (the cause), leaving enough room to fill in each cause of our resentments. Experience shows that when we write more than one column at a time, the process becomes too confusing. Once we have completed our first column, we move on to the next, remembering that we can always go back and make additions as other people, institutions, and principles toward which we hold resentments come to mind.

In **COLUMN 2**, for each person, institution, or principle listed in **COLUMN 1**, we write down the cause or causes for each resentment. For example:

COLUMN 1	COLUMN 2
People, institutions, or principles I'm resentful at	The cause or causes of each resentment
Mom	Puts too much pressure on me
	Enabled my addiction by looking the other way
	Embarrassed me in front of my friends
Dad	Belittled me
	Made me feel like I wasn't good enough
	Didn't defend me with Uncle Joe

In **COLUMN 3**, we identify how the "causes" listed in **COLUMN 2** affected our well-being—what part of us was hurt or threatened (Affects my . . .). For example:

COLUMN 1	COLUMN 2	COLUMN 3 Affects my . . .				
People, institutions, or principles I'm resentful at	The cause or causes of each resentment	Self-esteem	Security	Ambitions	Personal relationships	Sexual relationships
Mom	Puts too much pressure on me	X				
	Enabled my addiction by looking the other way	X	X	X		
	Embarrassed me in front of my friends	X			X	

Note that for each **COLUMN 2** cause, there can be more than one area affected. It is important to be thorough (which is one of the reasons we recommend attempting to finish each column before starting the next). Of course, if we think of things we've forgotten that belong in a previous column, we go back and add them. But again, we find it best to work on one column at a time and to be as exhaustive as possible.

In preparing to be rid of these resentments, we realize that the people who wronged us were perhaps spiritually sick. We say a prayer for each and every resentment. For example:

> _____ is a sick person. How can I be helpful to them? Higher Power, save me from being angry. Help me show _____ the same tolerance, kindness, and patience that I cheerfully grant a sick friend._

In **COLUMN 4**, we identify our part in each resentment. This means we look for what we did to create or aggravate the situations described in the earlier column. Where were we to blame? Sometimes this is obvious: when we resent a spouse or partner for being jealous, for example, we might easily see how our actions may have led to our partner's feelings. Other times, our part may be more difficult to identify. Perhaps our anger at a co-worker is completely understandable, based on how that person has treated us. In such a case, we may find that where we have failed is in our refusal to forgive: we have allowed the resentment to fester and grow, perhaps even gaining enjoyment out of it! Sometimes we rack our brains and cannot find our part in the resentment. This is where a sponsor's help can prove invaluable.

COLUMN 1	COLUMN 2	COLUMN 3					COLUMN 4				
		Affects my . . .					My part				
People, institutions, or principles I'm resentful at	The cause or causes of each resentment	Self-esteem	Security	Ambitions	Personal relationships	Sexual relationships	Selfish	Dishonest	Self-seeking	Frightened	Inconsiderate
Mom	Puts too much pressure on me	X					X	X			
	Enabled my addiction by looking the other way	X	X	X			X	X			X
	Embarrassed me in front of my friends	X			X			X		X	

Whenever you get stuck, take a break. These inventories take most of us weeks to complete—some of us have spent much longer, though such delay is not usually necessary. The sooner we begin, and the more we do each day, the sooner we will be finished. We find that when we return to working on our inventory after a break of more than a few minutes, it's a good idea to perform the willingness exercise (or prayer) again.

Once we have finished the fourth column of our Resentment Inventory, we look over our worksheet for things we may have missed or where we could have been more thorough.

We are now ready for the Fear Inventory.

Fear Inventory

The Fear Inventory is a lot like the Resentment Inventory, except we focus on our fears. We list each fear in **COLUMN 1**. When we have written out all of our fears to the best of our ability, we explore the cause or causes of our fears in **COLUMN 2**. In **COLUMN 3**, we write how each fear affects our lives today. In **COLUMN 4**, we write down our part, if any. For example:

COLUMN 1	COLUMN 2	COLUMN 3	COLUMN 4
I'm fearful of ...	What is the cause of my fear?	How does the fear affect my life?	What was my part, if any?
Heights	My brother pushed me off the second-floor balcony	Affects my ability to fly; my ambition to be a pilot	I bullied my brother

We then ask our Higher Power to remove the fear. We do this for each individual fear.

> Higher Power, please remove my fear of _____ and direct my attention toward what you would have me be.

Again, we should remember to take breaks and to take advantage of whatever prayers, tools, or techniques we have found that help us to be more willing, honest, and open-minded. For years, we have run away from ourselves, using marijuana to do so. Even without the marijuana, our tendency is to hide the truth rather than to face it. But if we are to grow as individuals, if we are to truly deal with this disease of marijuana addiction, we must face each of our fears so we can work through them. Remember, always, that we will not be working through them alone.

Once we have completed the Fear Inventory, we are ready for the Sex Inventory.

Sex Inventory

We begin the inventory of our own sex conduct by listing our current and past sexual partners in **COLUMN 1**. In **COLUMN 2**, we ask ourselves how we behaved toward each partner by answering questions such as

- Did we harm that person?
- Did we use them or take advantage of them?

As always, we try to be as honest and thorough as we can. Remember, we are not concerned here with what others may have done to us. If we have a resentment against someone because of something done to us, then we add that person to our Resentment Inventory.

In **COLUMN 3**, for each sexual partner, we ask ourselves the following question and check the boxes accordingly:

- Was I selfish, dishonest, and/or inconsiderate?

In **COLUMN 4**, for each sexual partner, we ask ourselves this question and check the boxes accordingly:

- Did I arouse jealousy, suspicion, and/or bitterness?

In **COLUMN 5**, we write down where we were at fault. In **COLUMN 6**, we describe what we could have done instead. Again, we always try to be thoroughly honest every step of the way. For example:

COLUMN 1	COLUMN 2	COLUMN 3 Was I selfish, dishonest, and/or inconsiderate?			COLUMN 4 Did I arouse jealousy, suspicion, and/or bitterness?			COLUMN 5	COLUMN 6
Sexual partners	Did I harm this person?	Selfish	Dishonest	Inconsiderate	Jealousy	Suspicion	Bitterness	Where was I at fault; what did I do?	What could I have done instead?
Pat	Yes	X			X			Made a scene; didn't listen	Talked it out calmly; paid more attention
Chris	No								
Jan	Yes		X		X			Lied	Told the truth

Step Four
Worksheets

Resentment Inventory

Instructions for Completion

Complete each column top to bottom before moving on to the next column. For example, fill in all the names of those you are resentful at before filling in the cause of each resentment.

COLUMN 1 We list people, institutions, or principles with whom we had a resentment.

COLUMN 2 We write the cause(s) of the resentment.

COLUMN 3 We identify the part of our life that was hurt or threatened. Was it our self-esteem, security, ambitions, personal relationships, or sexual relationships?

COLUMN 4 We identify the part we played in the resentment. Were we selfish, dishonest, self-seeking, frightened, or inconsiderate?

COLUMN 1	COLUMN 2	COLUMN 3 Affects my . . .					COLUMN 4 My part				
People, institutions, or principles I'm resentful at	The cause or causes of each resentment	Self-esteem	Security	Ambitions	Personal relationships	Sexual relationships	Selfish	Dishonest	Self-seeking	Frightened	Inconsiderate

Resentment Inventory (continued)

COLUMN 1	COLUMN 2	COLUMN 3 Affects my . . .					COLUMN 4 My part				
People, institutions, or principles I'm resentful at	The cause or causes of each resentment	Self-esteem	Security	Ambitions	Personal relationships	Sexual relationships	Selfish	Dishonest	Self-seeking	Frightened	Inconsiderate

Fear Inventory

Instructions for Completion

Complete each column from top to bottom before moving on to the next column.

COLUMN 1 *We list our fears thoroughly. We put them on paper, even though we had no resentment in connection with them.*
COLUMN 2 *We write down the cause of our fear.*
COLUMN 3 *We record how our fear affects our lives today.*
COLUMN 4 *We identify our part in the fear.*

COLUMN 1	COLUMN 2	COLUMN 3	COLUMN 4
I'm fearful of . . .	What is the cause of my fear?	How does the fear affect my life?	What was my part, if any?

Fear Inventory (continued)

COLUMN 1 I'm fearful of . . .	COLUMN 2 What is the cause of my fear?	COLUMN 3 How does the fear affect my life?	COLUMN 4 What was my part, if any?

Sex Inventory

Instructions for Completion

Complete each column from top to bottom before moving on to the next column.

COLUMN 1 *We list our sexual partners.*

COLUMN 2 *For each partner, we ask ourselves whether we harmed this person (writing "yes" or "no").*

COLUMN 3 *We identify whether we have been selfish, dishonest, and/or inconsiderate.*

COLUMN 4 *We identify whether we have aroused jealousy, suspicion, and/or bitterness.*

COLUMN 5 *We list where we were at fault, describing what we did.*

COLUMN 6 *We list what we could have done instead.*

COLUMN 1	COLUMN 2	COLUMN 3 Was I selfish, dishonest, and/or inconsiderate?			COLUMN 4 Did I arouse jealousy, suspicion, and/or bitterness?			COLUMN 5	COLUMN 6
	Did I harm this person?	Selfish	Dishonest	Inconsiderate	Jealousy	Suspicion	Bitterness	Where was I at fault; what did I do?	What could I have done instead?
Sexual partners									

Sex Inventory (continued)

COLUMN 1	COLUMN 2	COLUMN 3 Was I selfish, dishonest, and/or inconsiderate?			COLUMN 4 Did I arouse jealousy, suspicion, and/or bitterness?			COLUMN 5	COLUMN 6
		Selfish	Dishonest	Inconsiderate	Jealousy	Suspicion	Bitterness		
Sexual partners	Did I harm this person?							Where was I at fault; what did I do?	What could I have done instead?

Secrets and Other Issues Inventory

We may find that there are instances where we have harmed other people, lied, cheated, or stole. We may have secrets that we have yet to uncover. We list them now in the space below.

Assets Inventory

At this point, many of us have found it is important to take a look at the things we've done right. We look to see where we have had a positive impact on ourselves and others. We do this inventory so that we might have a more complete picture of ourselves. We also want to know those character traits and behaviors that we wish to foster in our lives.

What qualities do I have that I like?

We suggest looking over everything one more time, asking our Higher Power to help us find anything important we might have missed. If we have been exhaustive, if we have searched our hearts and souls, we may feel a sense of relief having completed this Step.

Discuss your Fourth Step work with your sponsor or a trusted fellow MA member.

We are now ready for **Step Five**.

Step Five

Admitted to God, to ourselves, and to another human being the exact nature of our wrongs.

Step Five requires courage and rigorous honesty. This Step continues the process begun in Step Four, uncovering things about ourselves of which we might not have been aware or were unwilling to face. Admitting what we find to our Higher Power, to ourselves, and to another human being helps us to overcome our feelings of shame, guilt, and embarrassment that may have kept us from realizing our true potential.

By the time we reach Step Five, many of us know with whom we will be sharing our Fourth Step inventory. Most commonly that person is a sponsor we have already chosen.

However, it's not imperative that you share your Fifth Step with your sponsor. *Life with Hope* suggests that a spiritual advisor or even a total stranger can hear your Fifth Step. (We have found it to be highly beneficial if the person has at least some understanding of the Twelve Step philosophy.)

The Fifth Step is about discovering patterns resulting from our resentments, fears, and selfishness. By identifying and sharing them, we find we can move beyond them.

Getting Started

- Read Step Five in *Life with Hope*. Note passages that are meaningful to you and statements or words that you don't understand.
- Look up dictionary definitions of the words you didn't understand.
- Look up the words *humility*, *humiliation*, and *honesty* in the dictionary; write out the definition(s) that you find significant, and write what each word means to you in the space below.

  Humility

  Humiliation

  Honesty

- Review Step Five in *Life with Hope* with your sponsor or a trusted fellow MA member.

Trust

1) Do I have a lack of trust in myself or others? Explain:

2) What factors, if any, contribute to my lack of trust?

Humility

3) What excuses, if any, do I use to avoid sharing my Step Four inventory?

4) Is there anything blocking me from having the courage to take this Step? Explain:

Many of us found it helpful to pray for *trust*, *humility*, and *courage*.

We now meet with our sponsor or spiritual advisor to share our Fourth Step inventories.

After Sharing

- After sharing our inventories, some of us have found it helpful to spend time alone in quiet reflection.
- If we discover any additional resentments, fears, or secrets, we share them with our sponsor or spiritual advisor at this time.

For many of us, after completing this Step, the wreckage of our past becomes a resource from which we can learn and grow. Many of us experience a new sense of empowerment, self-acceptance, integrity, and humility.

Discuss your Fifth Step work with your sponsor or a trusted fellow MA member.

We are now ready to move on to **Step Six**.

Notes for the Sponsor

Each sponsor develops their own approach to working with sponsees. That approach may vary from sponsee to sponsee and is almost certain to change over time.

Even without prior expertise, most sponsors are able to note patterns of thinking and behaving that are revealed by listening without judgment and keeping an open heart and mind.

Some of us may help our sponsees prepare a preliminary list of those to whom they might owe amends; others might leave that to the sponsees themselves. Likewise, some sponsors apply the same process to character defects. Still others do not include this process at all in the Fifth Step.

After a sponsee has shared their list, many sponsors have found it helpful to ask one final time if there are any other secrets that haven't been revealed or that didn't fit into any of the categories. This gentle prompting can help the sponsee dredge out any lingering "skeletons in the closet."

As a sponsor, you may find that while relief is a frequent result of taking this Step, anxiety and discomfort may also result from unearthing old memories and feelings. Sponsees may want to run away from what they've found. They may be tempted to avoid you because you "know too much." You may wish to help them resist these urges and turn to the experience of other addicts who are likely to reassure them with their own stories of struggle along this path.

The Fifth Step work that a sponsor and sponsee complete together is effective and often transformative. It may, however, also reveal certain issues or circumstances that the sponsor does not feel capable of handling. In most cases, the sponsor is not a qualified therapist. The sponsor may advise the sponsee to seek appropriate professional help such as a licensed counselor, a legal advisor, or a doctor. In some cases, even the sponsor may wish to seek outside advice, being mindful not to breach the special trust formed in the sponsor-sponsee relationship.

Many of us have found that our own sponsor is a great resource in working with a sponsee, though we must always be careful to maintain the confidentiality of our sponsee.

Step Six

Were entirely ready to have God remove all these defects of character.

Having completed Steps Four and Five, we now carry an awareness of the harm we have done to others and ourselves with more clarity and detail than ever before. In the patterns that emerged while sharing these details fully and openly for the first time, we have begun to recognize our defects of character.

Step Six says simply that we "Were entirely ready to have God remove all these defects of character." This Step requires that we practice the spiritual principles of willingness and faith. We need to be willing to let our Higher Power remove our defects of character and to have faith that when we are ready to let go, our Higher Power will be there to help us. Some defects of character we cannot wait to get rid of, while others we do not know how we can do without. This movement toward the new and unknown can be exciting and scary. On the one hand, we envision ourselves becoming more like how we always wanted to be and cannot wait to move on to the Seventh Step. On the other hand, we cannot imagine entirely letting go of some of our character traits, thus moving into an entirely new way of being.

Getting Started

- Read Step Six in *Life with Hope*. Note passages that are meaningful to you and statements or words that you don't understand.
- Look up dictionary definitions of the words you didn't understand.
- Look up the words *defect* and *willing* in the dictionary; write out the definition(s) that you find significant, and write what each word means to you in the space below.

Defect

Willing

- Review the word *faith* (from Step Three). Has your concept of faith changed at all? Explain:

- Review Step Six in *Life with Hope* with your sponsor or a trusted fellow MA member.

Willingness

1) List examples of times when you practiced the spiritual principle of willingness. What were the results?

Don't hesitate to use a notebook when more space is needed.

Example	Results
1.	
2.	
3.	
4.	
5.	
6.	
7.	

2) Do I have character defects that I can't wait to get rid of? If so, list them:

3) Do I have character defects that I can't imagine living without? If so, list them:

Faith

In letting go of our character defects, we can practice the same faith we used to stop using marijuana. We become willing to surrender our character defects.

4) List examples of times when you practiced the spiritual principle of faith. What were the results?

Don't hesitate to use a notebook when more space is needed.

Example	Results
1.	
2.	
3.	
4.	
5.	
6.	
7.	

5) Is there anything blocking me from having the courage to take this Step?

6) If my Higher Power is going to do all this for me, what's my job?

Character Defects

Many of us bristled at the words *character defect*. While we didn't claim to be perfect, the idea of having "defects" still made us think less of ourselves. Some of us use an alternative term, such as *character challenges*, as it's more encouraging and suggests that we can overcome them. With our diligence, our sponsor's guidance, and our Higher Power's help, many of us have found that we can indeed eventually lessen or free ourselves of many of the traits that no longer serve us. The changes begin as long as we are willing and have faith. By writing, sharing, and praying, we increase our readiness to let go of these character defects.

7) What are my character defects? Write down each defect and give a brief description of it.

Don't hesitate to use a notebook when more space is needed.

Character defect	Description
1.	
2.	
3.	
4.	
5.	
6.	
7.	

8) What are some examples of situations in which I acted on my defects?

9) How do my defects affect myself and others?

10) Do I have defects that I know I am attached to? Which ones are they?

11) Do I have defects that I think cannot be removed? Which ones are they?

12) What do I think would happen if these defects were removed?

13) What might I do in place of acting on these defects?

14) Do I trust my Higher Power to do what is best for me? Explain:

15) What would my life look like if each character defect were entirely removed?

Character defects are often rooted in normal and desirable human traits that have been allowed to run riot during our active addiction. Transformation comes when we examine these themes, for it is in the shadows of our worst traits that we may discover our greatest assets.

16) Can I connect any of my character defects to an underlying strength?

Don't hesitate to use a notebook when more space is needed.

Character defect	Underlying strength
1.	
2.	
3.	
4.	
5.	
6.	
7.	

17) What might happen if I were left with only the strengths, but not the character defect that grew from it?

It is widely acknowledged that working Step Six is an ongoing, even lifelong process. Many of us have experienced the dramatic lifting of some of our character defects, but few of us found that all of our defects were lifted at once, so we needed to accept that being ready also meant *staying* ready. This approach to the Sixth Step has been described as embracing a lifelong *Sixth Step attitude*: being constantly open to discovering our defects and surrendering them to a Higher Power.

Discuss your Sixth Step work with your sponsor or a trusted fellow MA member.

By practicing Step Six, we acquire the humility needed to take **Step Seven**.

Step Seven

Humbly asked God to remove our shortcomings.

The spiritual principle of Step Seven is humility. In this Step, we let go of our ego and humbly submit to a Power greater than ourselves so that our shortcomings may be removed. Step Seven doesn't mean that we think less of ourselves; it means we think of ourselves less.

Getting Started

- Read Step Seven in *Life with Hope*. Note passages that are meaningful to you and statements or words that you don't understand.
- Look up dictionary definitions of the words you didn't understand.
- Look up the words *humility* and *surrender* in the dictionary; write out the definition(s) that you find significant, and write what each word means to you in the space below.

Humility

Surrender

- Review Step Seven in *Life with Hope* with your sponsor or a trusted fellow MA member.

Humility

Humility is needed to calmly ask for help and to let go. We take the action and leave the results of our request to our Higher Power. Where humility once represented weakness to many of us, it now holds the key to serenity.

1) How do I feel about the idea of practicing humility?

2) How does humility affect my recovery?

3) What can I do to practice humility in this Step and in my daily life?

Surrender

Having faith that our Higher Power knows what is right for us requires a complete surrender. We need to get out of the way and allow the changes in our thinking and behaviors to happen.

4) How do I feel about surrendering and letting my Higher Power work in my life?

5) Am I willing to let go and surrender my character defects to my Higher Power? Why or why not?

Taking Action

Some form of prayer is customary when we ask our Higher Power to remove our shortcomings, but the spiritual path may vary. Some of us write our own prayer and keep it between our Higher Power and ourselves. Others share the experience with their sponsors, and others still invite members of their sponsorship "family tree" to share in the ritual. How we ask our Higher Power to remove our shortcomings is a personal choice. It is suggested that we make the choice with help from our sponsor or spiritual advisor.

This seemingly simple act of prayer gives our Higher Power permission to work in our lives. When something happens to trigger our character defects, we are more apt to recognize it and have an opportunity to seek help from our Higher Power.

6) How will I ask my Higher Power to remove my shortcomings?

7) How could I share the experience with my sponsor and other trusted members of the fellowship?

8) Do I believe that my Higher Power will remove my shortcomings? Why or why not?

Progress, Not Perfection

We often hear the phrase "progress, not perfection." Sometimes we make a little progress, and sometimes a lot. Any progress helps build the foundation for our recovery. When we strive for perfection, our ego gets in the way of letting our Higher Power into our recovery. It's important to take a step back. Looking at the progress we've made gives us an opportunity to see how much better our lives have become and how much our Higher Power has played a part. This is our recovery in action.

9) How do I practice perfection in my life?

10) How can I apply spiritual principles and the tools of recovery in situations when I attempt perfection?

11) What will I do when a character defect reoccurs in my life after I've asked my Higher Power to remove it?

As we ask our Higher Power to remove our character defects, we ask to transform them into new, useful patterns of thinking and behaving. When we ask humbly, we discover that our Higher Power can remove our imperfections and help us gain self-forgiveness.

Discuss your Seventh Step work with your sponsor or a trusted fellow MA member.

We are now ready to take **Step Eight**.

Step Eight

Made a list of all persons we had harmed,
and became willing to make amends to them all.

Step Eight incorporates honesty, openness, willingness, faith, acceptance, love, and forgiveness. This Step is about *becoming willing* to make amends, not actually making the amends. We look back and try to discover where we've been at fault. Having begun this work in Step Four, we identify all the people we have harmed and in what ways.

Although we may be tempted to rush out and make our amends, it's important for us to remember that Step Eight is merely making a list. If we try to make amends without our sponsor's guidance and a plan, we may end up doing more harm than good.

Getting Started

- Read Step Eight in *Life with Hope.* Note passages that are meaningful to you and statements or words that you don't understand.

- Look up dictionary definitions of the words you didn't understand.

- Look up the words *amends* and *forgiveness* in the dictionary; write out the definition(s) that you find significant, and write what each word means to you in the space below.

  Amends

  Forgiveness

- Review your definition of the word *willing* and what it meant to you from Step Six (in this workbook). Has its meaning changed for you at all since you worked that Step? Explain:

- Review Step Eight in *Life with Hope* with your sponsor or a trusted fellow MA member.

Willingness

Some of us need to begin by praying for help to become willing to make our list. Staying focused on that objective is often very helpful.

1) Am I willing to make my list? Why or why not?

2) Are there any resentments preventing me from being willing to make amends? If so, list them below.

3) Is it possible to let go of those resentments now? If not, can I add those names to my list anyway and work toward becoming willing later? Explain:

4) What might help me to become more willing?

5) Are there amends I need to make that might cause harm to myself or others? If so, list them here.

6) What concerns and/or fears am I having about making amends?

Writing Our List

We write down whom we have harmed as a result of our character defects and precisely how we harmed them. We categorize our list according to those we feel should receive **IMMEDIATE** amends, those we are willing to approach **SOON**, those we will approach **LATER**, and those we **CANNOT IMAGINE EVER** being willing to approach. Our list may include people who have passed away or those we have little chance of locating. We may also want to add ourselves to the list.

We write down the harm we have caused spiritually, socially, mentally, physically, and financially. For example:

Spiritually
- Did we force others to adhere to our beliefs without respect for theirs?
- Did we use sarcasm or other means to undercut others' beliefs?

Socially
- Did we hurt others to feel superior, or did we act passively to gain control?
- Did we isolate from our family and friends?

Mentally
- Did we maliciously toy with other people's minds?
- Were we neglectful, manipulative, or exploitive?

Physically
- Did we abuse others or let others abuse us (or our children)?
- Did we sexually harm or cheat on someone?
- Did we try to do our best, or did we do just enough to get by?

Financially
- Were we careless and wasteful or greedy and miserly?
- Did we deprive others of necessities?
- Did we cheat or steal from others?

Wherever possible, we write down what we might do to set things straight with the people on our list. Where applicable, we identify what might stop us from making amends to a particular person. (See next page for worksheet.)

Discuss your Eighth Step work with your sponsor or a trusted fellow MA member.

It may be that we are not responsible for some of the harm we include on our list. Reviewing each potential amend with our sponsor or spiritual advisor is essential. They can help us gain insight, strength, hope, and the *forgiveness* necessary to proceed to **Step Nine**.

Don't hesitate to use a notebook when more space is needed.

Preparing for My Amends

Whom I have harmed	How I harmed them	Categorize my amends list by willingness				What I might do to set things straight	What might stop me from making amends
		Immediate	Soon	Later	Not willing		

Step Nine

Made direct amends to such people wherever possible,
except when to do so would injure them or others.

Step Nine is an action Step. By taking the information we've acquired in the first eight Steps, we begin the process of making amends. We continue the work begun in Step Four—cleaning up the wreckage of our past. The Ninth Step is about our admission of wrongful conduct, a sincere apology, and reasonable reparation. There are many approaches to this Step. Ultimately, how we choose to accomplish it will be a personal choice, guided by our sponsor or spiritual advisor.

The purpose of Step Nine is not to win the admiration of others, but to restore our self-esteem and further our spiritual growth. The form of our amends may vary, but our attitude is always the same—willingness to take responsibility for our behavior and taking action to right our wrongs.

Although many of us approached this Step with hesitation, we found it to be one of the most deeply rewarding and spiritual experiences of our lives.

Getting Started

- Read Step Nine in *Life with Hope*. Note passages that are meaningful to you and statements or words that you don't understand.
- Look up dictionary definitions of the words you didn't understand.
- Look up the words *justice*, *integrity*, and *reparation* in the dictionary; write out the definition(s) that you find significant, and write what each word means to you in the space below.

Justice

Integrity

Reparation

- Review Step Nine in *Life with Hope* with your sponsor or a trusted fellow MA member.

Preparation

Many of us have found it helpful to begin by writing letters to each person on our list and reviewing them with our sponsors. This helps ensure that we keep the focus on ourselves and not blame others for our actions. It prevents us from beginning with a sincere apology and ending up with the "yeah, buts." For example: "Yeah, I stole your money, but you were cheap."

When beginning our letters, it is suggested we come clean about our addiction, whenever possible, not as an excuse but as a potential explanation of our behavior. We make amends for what we have not done as well as for what we have done—such as isolating and neglecting others.

In some cases, we make amends to those who have harmed us, maybe even more than we harmed them. The Ninth Step is about clearing up our side of the street, not taking the inventory of others.

Taking Action/Making Amends

Whenever possible, we make our amends face-to-face. Some of us use our letters as a script, to make sure we say exactly what we mean to say when making our actual amends. However, using the phone, mail, or email is sometimes our only option.

In some cases, making amends might do more harm than good. Again, that is something to be discussed and decided on with the guidance of our sponsor. Concern about consequences does not excuse us from making amends, unless to do so would injure them or others. When we owe financial amends to practicing addicts, we seek options for our safety so we do not put ourselves at risk for relapse and illegality by being in the proximity of drugs.

Sometimes making direct amends isn't possible. If the person we have harmed has died or is untraceable, we can write a letter and read it to our sponsor and then make an indirect or living amends. Such amends can include contributing to charities, doing volunteer work, or making an honest change in our behavior toward others.

The Ninth Step is about taking responsibility for our actions. We acknowledge where something we've done or said has caused harm to others. We are facing our past and owning our part. We make our amends and leave the results to our Higher Power.

Discuss your Ninth Step work with your sponsor or a trusted fellow MA member.

The rewards we receive from taking this Step are profound and sublime. Miracles become an everyday reality. The hard work we put into the first nine Steps is a valuable gift. In order to keep that gift, we turn to **Step Ten**.

Step Ten

*Continued to take personal inventory
and when we were wrong, promptly admitted it.*

Step Ten is the beginning of the "maintenance" Steps, combining what we have learned in the first nine Steps and putting that knowledge to work on a daily basis. Coupled with Steps Eleven and Twelve, Step Ten is about our continued commitment to spiritual progress. Taking a daily personal inventory enables us to maintain our self-reflection and awareness, and ensures our ongoing growth in recovery. As we gain an understanding of our thoughts and actions (as well as their consequences), and willingly correct ourselves, our lives are transformed.

Getting Started

- Read Step Ten in *Life with Hope*. Note passages that are meaningful to you and statements or words that you don't understand.

- Look up dictionary definitions of the words you didn't understand.

- Look up the words *promptly*, *perseverance*, and *commitment* in the dictionary; write out the definition(s) that you find significant, and write what each word means to you in the space below.

Promptly

Perseverance

Commitment

- Review Step Ten in *Life with Hope* with your sponsor or a trusted fellow MA member.

The Daily Inventory

It is suggested that we get into a routine of daily self-reflection. Some of us have found it helpful to pick a time of day when we can sit quietly and review the previous twenty-four hours. We might choose to do this exercise before going to bed at night, or we might prefer to examine the previous day first thing in the morning. The time of day doesn't have to be the same, but doing the exercise at the same general time each day helps to establish a habit. While a daily moral inventory may be done in written form, a mental list is also helpful as this practice is integrated into everyday life.

This is an ongoing process. We strive for progress, not perfection. Many days we don't handle everything as we'd wished, and it's important that we forgive ourselves if we fall short of our own expectations. This is not a test; there are no right or wrong answers. These are ideals we're striving for, rather than a checklist of perfectionism.

We didn't get to the Tenth Step in one day. Self-mastery is a process, not an event. Easy does it.

We consider these questions, aware that some days not all of them will apply:

☐ Did I stay sober today?

☐ Did I pray or meditate?

☐ Did I pray for someone else?

☐ Did I talk to my sponsor today?

☐ Did I go to a meeting?

☐ Did I read any Twelve Step literature?

☐ What Steps did I consciously work today?

☐ Did I do anything to help my recovery?

☐ Did I learn anything about myself today?

☐ Did my disease influence my life today?

☐ Was I fearful? If so, about what?

☐ Was I obsessed about anything today? If so, what?

☐ Was I honest?

☐ Did I worry about yesterday or tomorrow?

☐ Did I gossip today?

☐ Did my resentments lead me to do things I regretted?

☐ Was I overly emotional?

☐ Was I judgmental, prejudicial, or unfairly discriminating?

☐ Did I have a negative attitude and inflict it upon those around me?

☐ Was I tolerant and open-minded?

☐ Was my attitude loving and forgiving?

☐ Was I good to myself today? If so, how?

☐ Was I kind to someone else today? If so, how?

☐ Did I give of myself today without expecting anything in return?

☐ Have I expressed gratitude to my Higher Power for everything that went right today?

☐ Did I make any mistakes today? Did I promptly admit them and make amends, if appropriate?

☐ Do I have any unfinished business to address tomorrow?

Discuss your Tenth Step work with your sponsor or a trusted fellow MA member.

Daily practice of Step Ten helps restore us to sanity by keeping us on the best terms possible with the world around us. We begin to truly experience peace and serenity. We are now ready to improve our conscious contact with our Higher Power. To do that, we focus on **Step Eleven**.

Step Eleven

Sought through prayer and meditation to improve our
conscious contact with God, *as we understood God,* *praying only for*
knowledge of God's will for us and the power to carry that out.

Step Eleven is about nurturing and improving our relationship with the Higher Power of our understanding and increasing our spiritual awareness. Many of us have found that when we pray for knowledge of God's will for us, we discover the right actions to take and the right words to say. Like Steps Ten and Twelve, the Eleventh Step is one we don't have to wait to work.

One of the challenges of the Eleventh Step is learning how to understand the difference between God's will and self-will. We need only ask for our Higher Power's guidance and wisdom to be assured that our own desires are not the focus. The more we let go of our wish list, the more we allow our Higher Power to work in our lives. As we experience the power of prayer and meditation in our lives, our awareness grows stronger and our faith deepens.

Getting Started

- Read Step Eleven in *Life with Hope*. Note passages that are meaningful to you and statements or words that you don't understand.

- Look up dictionary definitions of the words you didn't understand.

- Look up the words *prayer, meditation,* and *spiritual* in the dictionary; write out the definition(s) that you find significant, and write what each word means to you in the space below.

Prayer

Meditation

Spiritual

- Review Step Eleven in *Life with Hope* with your sponsor or a trusted fellow MA member.

Prayer

Some of us begin and end our day thanking our Higher Power for another day clean and sober. Others use formal prayers from recovery literature, organized religion, or other spiritual practices. Many talk directly from their hearts, letting God know their innermost thoughts and feelings. Any method we choose will yield positive results. Over time, we usually find that communication with our Higher Power becomes easier and allows for a deeper relationship to develop.

In addition to praying for knowledge of God's will for us, we also pray for the "power to carry that out." We may become aware of God's will, but due to many factors, we may feel unable to follow through. In order to successfully work the Eleventh Step, it becomes necessary to practice the spiritual principle of faith and to trust God's will in our daily life. If we focus on being grateful for the things that are good in our lives, the desire to carry out God's will becomes easier.

Practice of Prayer
Questions for your consideration:

- What method(s) of prayer have I tried?
- Which, if any, works best for me?
- Have I felt a connection to my Higher Power?
- Have I found that any of my prayers have been answered (such as relief from the obsession to use or help in taking the next right action)?
- Have I been able to establish a daily practice of prayer?
- If not, is there anything I might do to help me integrate prayer more easily into my life?

Meditation

Just as prayer is a form of talking to God, meditation is a form of listening to God. Meditation techniques are designed to help us develop the ability to be aware of our Higher Power. Some prefer guided meditations; others practice moving meditations; still others prefer simple breathing techniques. No matter which form of meditation we perform, the process of quieting the mind further develops our awareness and our connection to our Higher Power.

Some meditation methods suggest that we pay attention to our breath as a way of quieting our mind. For some of us, repeating a phrase of a spiritual nature, such as "Let go and let God," and staying focused on the words can help calm our mind. When our minds wander, as they invariably will, we gently and lovingly bring them back into focus. With all techniques, we need a constant process of refocusing our awareness when it becomes distracted. With regular practice, the ability to focus and maintain our awareness increases. As we calm our minds, our intuition grows; serenity and solutions come to us.

Meditation Techniques
Questions for your consideration:

- Which, if any, meditation techniques have worked for me? How have they worked?
- Have I made progress toward developing a regular meditation practice?
- Have I noticed any changes in my ability to meditate since entering recovery?
- In what ways, if any, have I or my life changed as a result of meditation?

As we improve our ability to stay in conscious contact with our Higher Power, we develop a greater understanding of self-love, inner peace, true joy, and happiness. We intuitively know what to do in the moment; our guidance comes from our Higher Power. If we maintain this connection, we'll remain in harmony with God's will for us.

Conscious Contact
Questions for your consideration:

- Have I experienced moments of conscious contact with my Higher Power?
- How do I know when I've achieved a conscious contact with my Higher Power?
- What factors help me do this?
- What gets in the way of my attaining a conscious contact with God?
- How do I know God's will for me? Do I always know? Sometimes know? Never know?
- What, if anything, is blocking me from carrying out God's will?
- How can I help myself carry out my Higher Power's will for me in all areas of my life?

Discuss your Eleventh Step work with your sponsor or a trusted fellow MA member.

Step Eleven allows us the strength and courage to incorporate the program in all aspects of our lives. We're now able to be of help and service to others, which leads us to **Step Twelve**.

Step Twelve

*Having had a spiritual awakening as the result of these steps,
we tried to carry this message to marijuana addicts
and to practice these principles in all our affairs.*

Step Twelve promises us that if we honestly and thoroughly apply the first eleven Steps in our lives, we will achieve a spiritual awakening. Through this awakening, with the help of our Higher Power and the tools of the program, we are given the gift of recovery.

Getting Started

- Read Step Twelve in *Life with Hope.* Note passages that are meaningful to you and statements or words that you don't understand.

- Look up dictionary definitions of the words you didn't understand.

- Look up the words *service* and *result* in the dictionary; write out the definition(s) that you find significant, and write what each word means to you in the space below.

Service

Result

- Review Step Twelve in *Life with Hope* with your sponsor or a trusted fellow MA member.

Service

This Step is about the concept of service, an essential part of our recovery and of MA as a whole. Without service, there would be no program. Having been spared from active addiction, we are free to help other addicts and give back what has been so freely given to us.

We begin to work the Twelfth Step as soon as we enter the rooms. We are of service to others when we attend meetings, reach out to newcomers, talk with members on the phone, take service commitments, and sponsor fellow addicts. The more we help others, the more we help ourselves.

1) How have I been of service?

2) How do I carry the message of recovery?

Practicing the Principles

Each Step carries at least one main spiritual principle. We strive to apply these principles not only to the program and the people in it, but to all aspects of our lives. Look up the meaning of each principle in the dictionary and write it in the space provided.

The principle	The meaning of the principle
Step 1 HONESTY	
Step 2 HOPE	
Step 3 FAITH	
Step 4 COURAGE	
Step 5 INTEGRITY	
Step 6 WILLINGNESS	
Step 7 HUMILITY	
Step 8 LOVE AND FORGIVENESS	
Step 9 JUSTICE	
Step 10 PERSEVERANCE	
Step 11 SPIRITUAL AWARENESS	
Step 12 SERVICE	

In All Our Affairs

Questions for your consideration:

- How do I practice each spiritual principle in my life today?
- If I don't already practice a particular principle, how might I begin?
- What, if anything, stands in my way of practicing these principles?

It is essential that we take *all* of the Steps and practice *all* of the principles if we are to maintain our recovery. In order for us to keep what we've been given, we need to give it away. If we closely examine our evolving relationship with our Higher Power, ourselves, and others, we can see a definite shift in our attitudes and perceptions. As we make spiritual progress, we gain inner strength, self-esteem, and serenity. We can look at our part in every situation and be willing to do whatever it takes to practice the principles of this program.

3) What benefits have I experienced as a result of working these Steps?

4) Have I experienced a spiritual awakening? If so, how has it manifested?

5) How has living the principles affected my daily life?

As we continue to be of service and to practice these principles in all our affairs, we are transformed from suffering addicts into people who are able to be happy, joyous, and free.

Discuss your Twelfth Step work with your sponsor or a trusted fellow MA member.

We take these Steps for ourselves, not by ourselves. Others have gone before; others will follow. **We recover.**

Notes

Notes

Notes